SUN and STORMS

Canadian Summer Weather

Nicole Mortillaro

Scholastic Canada Ltd.

Toronto New York London Auckland Sydney
Mexico City New Delhi Hong Kong Buenos Aires

For Sara, Scott and my family.

Photo Credits

Page iv: Juan Silva/Getty Images; Page 2: Dave Reede/First Light™; Page 3: Detail, courtesy George Kourounis; Page 8: Corbis/First Light™; Page 9: Detail, courtesy Marc Nagy; Page 14: Courtesy Pascal Desjardins; Page 16 and back cover: Courtesy James Koole; Page 17: Courtesy Le Groupe Madie Solution Publicité; Page 18: Courtesy James Koole; Page 19: Detail, courtesy Art Houghton; Page 20: Courtesy Marc Nagy; Page 22: Courtesy Wayne Roraph; Page 25 (upper and inset): Courtesy the National Oceanic and Atmospheric Administration Photo Library, NOAA Central Library; OAR/ERL/National Severe Storms Laboratory (NSSL); Page 26: Courtesy George Kourounis; Page 27: Courtesy Chad Zallas; Page 28: Courtesy the National Oceanic and Atmospheric Administration Photo Library, NOAA Central Library; OAR/ERL/ National Severe Storms Laboratory (NSSL); Page 29: Courtesy Robert den Hartigh; Page 32: Courtesy Environment Canada; Page 33: Courtesy the Edmonton Sun, Dan Riedlhuber; Page 36: Image courtesy of MODIS Rapid Response Project at NASA/GSFC; Page 37: Detail, courtesy Marc Nagy; Page 39: Courtesy the National Oceanic and Atmospheric Administration; Page 40: Courtesy Roger Percy and Andre Laflamme, Environment Canada; Page 41: Courtesy Environment Canada; Page 43: Courtesy the National Aeronautics and Space Administration; Page 45: Courtesy the National Aeronautics and Space Administration; Page 46: Courtesy Eldon Griffiths; Page 47: Detail, courtesy George Kourounis; Page 50: Courtesy Roger Lemire, reproduction authorized by Les Publications du Québec; Page 53: Glenbow 2496-4; Page 54 and 55: Courtesy Environment Canada; Page 56: Courtesy the CN Tower

Special thanks to Geoff Coulson, Warning Preparedness Meteorologist with Environment Canada, and to Dr. David Sills, Severe Weather Scientist, Cloud Physics and Severe Weather Research Division, Meteorological Service of Canada, for their helpful advice and expertise.

Diagrams by Erik Jezerano.

National Library of Canada Cataloguing in Publication

Mortillaro, Nicole, 1972-

Sun and storms : Canadian summer weather / Nicole Mortillaro.

(Canada close up)
ISBN 0-439-95745-1

1. Summer—Canada—Juvenile literature. 2. Canada—Climate—Juvenile literature. I. Title. II. Series: Canada close up (Markham, Ont.)

QC981.3.M67 2005   j551.6971   C2004-905850-9

Table of Contents

Pronunciation Guide

We've given you a guide on how to say some of the new words you
will find in this book. The syllable that's in **bold** type is stressed,
or said a little louder than the others. Here is a key to the vowel
sounds in this book:

a as in at; **ay** as in day; **ee** as in see; **o** as in ocean; **oo** as in food;
u as in but; **i** as in pit; **ah** as in pot; **ow** as in pout

Introduction

A lot of people think that Canada's weather is always cold and snowy. But that's not true. We get a lot more than just snow. Every summer Canada has heat waves, tornadoes and floods. Sometimes we even get hurricanes!

For many Canadians, summer is their favourite season. That's because when it is warm out, there are lots of things we can do outside. We can go swimming, ride our bikes or go to the park.

Summer weather also helps things grow. Our plants and grass need the rain and warm sun to get bigger. So do we!

Chapter 1

Sun and Wind

Have you ever noticed that people
always talk about the weather?
That's because weather is
something we all share.
Since it is always changing,
it also gives us lots to talk about.

But what is weather? Weather is the change in things like temperature, rain and wind in a certain place, over a short time.

Our weather is changing every day, every hour and even every minute! It might get warmer or cooler. It might get sunnier or cloudier. The Sun causes these changes. It even helps make wind and rain.

The heat from the Sun warms the ground and the air in our **atmosphere** [at-mu-sfeer].

The atmosphere is something you can't see, but it's always there. It acts like a heavy blanket that protects our planet. It is made up of many gases, including water vapour, and tiny particles. It keeps heat and air in a layer around Earth.

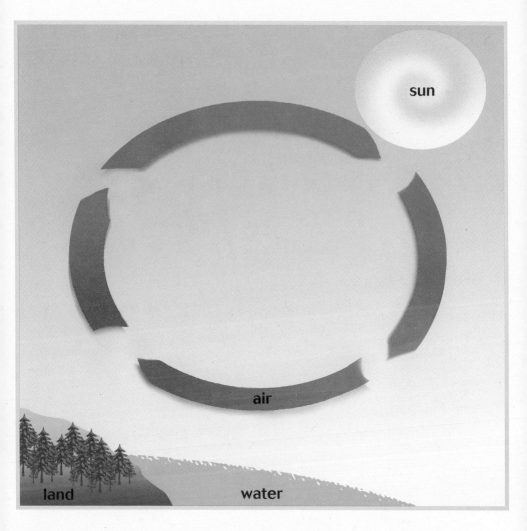

Warm air rises and cold air comes in to take its place. As the warm air rises, it cools again and then drops. Air is always moving across our planet. That's what wind is.

When the Sun warms up Earth's surface, air above the ground gets warmer too.

This warm air rises, and cold air comes in to take its place. As the warm air rises in the atmosphere, it cools and drops again. Because air can't rise and fall in the same place, the rising warm air and the falling cool air push each other sideways. This causes air to move across our planet and become wind.

We have different seasons because our planet moves around the Sun. And as it moves, it also spins.

But Earth doesn't sit up straight, like a top. As it spins, it tilts a little. So sometimes one part of Earth is tilted toward the sun. That part gets the sun's rays straight on.

When the sun's rays hit our part of the world this way, we get warmer weather. When we are tilted away from the Sun, it is colder.

When more direct sunlight hits Canada, it's summertime!

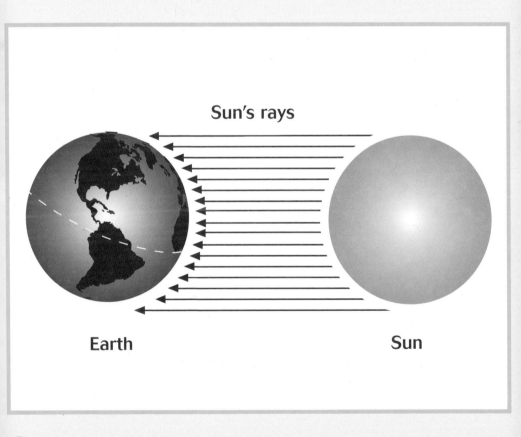

Sun's rays

Earth

Sun

When more of the sun's rays directly hit Canada, we get warmer weather.

Chapter 2

Rain and Clouds

Have you ever wanted to play outside, but couldn't because it was raining? You might have been upset, but we need rain.

Just like the Sun, rain helps things grow. Everything on Earth needs water to survive — even us!

Just think how you feel when you haven't had anything to drink. You get pretty thirsty, right? So do plants and animals when they don't get enough rain.

Rain comes from clouds. But how does it get there? Try a little experiment. On a hot day, pour a glass of water onto the sidewalk. After an hour, go outside to where you poured it. You won't see the water anymore. Where did it go?

The heat from the sun turned the liquid into a gas called **water vapour**. This process is called **evaporation** [ee-**vap**-o-ray-shun].

When water vapour rises high into our atmosphere, it cools and changes back to tiny water droplets.

These droplets collect together with things like dust particles to make the clouds we see.

When the water droplets get large enough, they fall from the cloud and we get rain.

cools and forms clouds

falls as rain

water evaporates

When water from oceans, lakes and rivers evaporates, it turns into water vapour. The water vapour rises in our atmosphere where it cools. This turns the vapour back into water droplets and gives us rain.

The clouds in the sky can tell us a lot about the weather. Here are some of the most common types of cloud.

Cumulus
[**kyoo**-myoo-lus]
These are the puffy clouds you see on a nice day. They don't bring rain. But sometimes they can grow into cumulonimbus clouds.

Cumulonimbus
[kyoo-myoo-lo-**nim**-bus]
These clouds rise high into the sky. They are puffy with a flat top. They can bring heavy rain, lightning and thunder.

Cirrus
[**see**-rus]
These high clouds are thin and wispy. Some people call these clouds "mare's tails." They usually mean good weather.

Nimbostratus

[nim-bo-**stra**-tus]

These are usually dark grey clouds. They can bring light rain or snow.

Stratus

[**stra**-tus]

These layered clouds usually cover the whole sky. They can sometimes bring light rain.

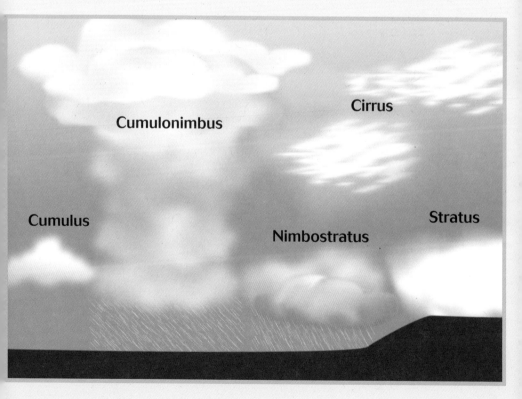

Cirrus

Cumulonimbus

Cumulus

Stratus

Nimbostratus

Some of the most common types of cloud

The light we see from the Sun is made up of many colours. Sometimes when the Sun comes out after a storm, its light goes through the water droplets in the air. The water droplets separate the colours in the light. That's when we see rainbows!

Rain is good for everybody and everything on Earth. But what happens when we get too much rain? It can mean trouble.

It's like running water in a bathtub that's not plugged. If you turn the tap on too high, the water can't go down the drain fast enough.
The tub may start to overflow.
This happens to our planet, too.

If it rains too much we get floods. The ground can't soak up all that water fast enough. Our rivers and lakes rise. This can be very dangerous.

Floods can sweep away cars and even entire houses. People have to make sure that they go to higher ground when a flood begins.

Floodwaters can move very fast, and they don't have to be deep to knock a person over.

That is why it's important to stay away from rivers when it has rained a lot.

A cloud brings rain to a city.

In 1996 Saguenay, Quebec, had one of the worst floods in Canadian history. The floods were powerful enough to sweep away a whole shopping centre!

Chapter 3

Thunder and Lightning

Canada gets most of its thunderstorms in the summer.

Thunderstorms can be scary. Bad ones can bring strong winds and hail. But many people find thunderstorms exciting and beautiful too. They bring lightning, thunder and the rain we need.

There are three parts to a thunderstorm.

1. If there is the right mix of dry, cold air high in the sky and warm, moist air near the ground, a cumulus cloud begins to grow very fast. This is the first part of the storm.

A cumulonimbus cloud grows from a cumulus cloud.

2. In the second part of a thunderstorm, the cloud rises high in the sky. It also becomes flat on top. It is now a cumulonimbus cloud. When you see this cloud, a storm is being made!

Billions of drops of water collect inside the cloud. The cloud gets so full of water that sunlight can't get through. That's why the cloud gets dark.

Inside the cloud, water droplets and tiny pieces of ice begin to crash together. This leads to lightning and thunder. The water droplets grow. When they get too heavy, it begins to rain.

3. The third part is the end of the storm. The rain stops. The cloud gets smaller.

Lightning can be fun to watch, but it's also very dangerous. Every year lightning kills six to ten people in Canada. It also causes more than half of all forest fires.

● In 2004 lightning in British Columbia started over 400 fires. They spread very quickly. This is because the thunderstorm didn't have enough rain to put out the fires. Many people had to leave their homes. Many of their houses burned down.

What is lightning? Have you ever rubbed your feet on a carpet and touched someone? What happened? You gave off an electric shock. That's because rubbing the carpet built up static electricity in your body.

Static electricity is electricity that is looking for a place to go. When you touched the other person, it passed through you and shocked them.

Lightning is made the same way. Water droplets and ice in a cloud bump around. This makes static electricity. This electricity will try to jump to something else. Most of the time it jumps to another cloud. But sometimes it jumps to the ground, and that's what we call lightning.

Lightning also causes the sound we call thunder. When lightning flashes, the air around it gets very hot, very fast. This makes the air expand quickly. When this happens, it causes a sound wave.

If the thunder sounds crackly, the storm is close. If the thunder sounds rumbly, the storm is far away.

Sometimes during a thunderstorm, hail will begin to fall. Hail is balls of ice that fall from a storm cloud. They are made when water droplets attach to dust particles in the atmosphere. The water freezes and falls. Then the wind carries it up into the cloud again where it is very cold. This happens many times.

Finally the hail gets too heavy for the cloud to hold and it falls to earth. That's why if you cut open a hailstone, you will see many layers.

Hail can cause a lot of damage. It can wreck cars, homes and even crops. Almost every year Canadian farmers lose some of their crops because hail has damaged them. If you hear or see hail, run inside! You don't want to get hit with it.

The strong winds of a storm can be dangerous too.
In 1999, a sudden storm in Ontario overturned cars and
damaged buildings.

In July 2004 a strong thunderstorm hit Edmonton, Alberta. Heavy rains flooded parts of the city. The West Edmonton Mall had its roof damaged by hail. People came out of the mall to find their cars almost under water. All the hail made the area look as if it was the middle of winter!

Chapter 4

Tornadoes

One of the scariest things that a strong thunderstorm can bring is a tornado.

Most of us have never seen a tornado, but Canada records about 80 a year!

Tornadoes usually happen during a really bad thunderstorm. For a tornado to form, there needs to be the right mixture of temperature, moisture and wind.

All thunderstorms have warm, moist air that quickly rises from the ground. When the winds change speed and direction in just the right way, the rising warm air can begin to spin. This spinning motion can make a funnel cloud at the bottom of the thunderstorm.

Not all funnel clouds touch the ground, but those that do are called tornadoes. In some tornadoes, the bottom part of the funnel cloud is invisible. So it may not look like it is touching the ground, but it is.

A tornado acts like a big vacuum cleaner that sucks up everything in its path. It picks up dust, dirt and anything else that gets in its way.

● The spinning winds of a tornado can suck up almost everything in their path.

Most tornadoes aren't very big, but they cause a lot of damage. They come in different shapes and sizes. Some people also call tornadoes "twisters."

Canada has had some very bad tornadoes. On May 31, 1985, the city of Barrie, Ontario, was hit by a powerful tornado. It destroyed many houses. A lot of people were seriously hurt, and some even died.

● In July 2000 a campground in Pine Lake, Alberta, was hit by a horrible tornado. Trailers flipped over and trees were ripped out of the ground. Many people were hurt, and some were killed. Four-month-old Ashley Thomson was ripped out of her car seat and sucked up as high as a three-storey building. But she landed a few hundred metres away with only a cut foot. Some people called her the miracle baby.

In Canada, tornadoes usually happen between May and September. We get most of them between June and July. Tornados are most likely in Ontario, Saskatchewan, Alberta and Manitoba.

Meteorologists [mee-tee-o-**rahl**-u-jists] are scientists who study and predict the weather. They use a scale to measure how strong a tornado was. It is called the Fujita Scale. It was created by meteorologist Dr. Tetsuya Fujita.

During a strong thunderstorm, meteorologists may issue a **tornado watch** or a **tornado warning**.

Fujita Scale

F0: winds of 64-116 km/h – damage to trees, roofs.

F1: winds of 117-180 km/h – cars turned over; trees pulled up out of the ground.

F2: winds of 181-252 km/h – roofs blown off houses; mobile homes destroyed.

F3: winds of 253-330 km/h – metal buildings fall; forest or farmlands flattened.

F4: winds of 331-417 km/h – few building walls left standing.

F5: winds of 418-509 km/h – homes destroyed or carried away (very rare). Some people think Canada has never had one of these.

There are things you can do to keep safe during a tornado.

1. Stay away from all windows.

2. If you have a basement, go there.

3. If you don't, lie in a bathtub with a mattress or pillow over your head. This will help protect you from everything that flies around in a tornado.

A tornado watch means that a tornado could happen. A tornado warning means that a tornado is starting to develop. When you hear one of these warnings, go inside.

Because a tornado sucks up everything in its path, its winds are full of broken pieces of buildings, branches and sometimes even large objects like cars! This is called **debris** [di-**bree**] and it is one of the most dangerous parts of a tornado.

Nova Scotia

Chapter 5

Hurricanes

Hurricanes are like tornadoes, but they need to begin over warm water. They are also much stronger than tornadoes.

Hurricanes take a long time to form. First they start as storms.

For a storm to become a hurricane, it needs:

◉ warm ocean water
◉ warm, moist air
◉ winds high above Earth that are moving the same way as the winds close to the water
◉ something to spin the storm

Warm ocean waters give a hurricane its energy. Earth's rotation helps to give the storm its spin. When the winds become very fast (more than 118 km per hour), we call the storm a hurricane.

When a hurricane hits land, it starts to get weaker. That is because there isn't any more warm water to give it energy.

Hurricanes can't form near Canada. Our waters are too cold. But we still get them.

That's because hurricanes can travel far. They often last for days, or even weeks. So a hurricane may start over warm waters far south of Canada, but over time it can move north and reach the Atlantic provinces. Once it hits land, it can be very dangerous to the people who live in its path.

This photo taken in 2004 shows Hurricane Jeanne, Hurricane Karl and Tropical Storm Lisa over the Atlantic Ocean.

Canada's Atlantic provinces get about four hurricanes a year. Most hurricanes weaken as they travel north, but their winds can still cause a lot of damage.

● In 2003 Hurricane Juan hit Nova Scotia. Many people were hurt and eight people died. Over 100 million trees were destroyed! The biggest wave recorded at that time was nine metres. That's as tall as a three-storey house!

Even when hurricanes lose their strength, they can still be dangerous. In 1954 what was left of Hurricane Hazel hit Ontario. Even though it was no longer a hurricane, eighty-one people died in floods because of the storm and its heavy rains.

Just like they do for tornadoes, meteorologists use a scale to measure how strong a hurricane is. It is called the Saffir-Simpson scale. It is named after Herbert Saffir and Dr. Robert Simpson.

Saffir-Simpson Scale

Category 1: winds of 118-153 km/h – damage to trees and unanchored mobile homes.

Category 2: winds of 154-177 km/h – some trees blown down; major damage to mobile homes; some damage to roofs of buildings; flooding.

Category 3: winds of 178-210 km/h – large trees blown down; mobile homes destroyed; some damage to small buildings; flooding.

Category 4: winds of 211-249 km/h – signs blown down; damage to roofs, windows, and doors; complete destruction of mobile homes; serious flooding.

Category 5: winds over 249 km/h – bad damage to windows and doors; damage to roofs; small buildings flipped and blown away; serious flooding; bad damage to homes near the coast.

Hurricane Frances forms over the Atlantic Ocean in 2004.

Hurricanes bring many dangerous things. There are storm surges, strong winds and heavy rainfall.

A **storm surge** is when water along the coast rises very high. This happens because the winds are pushing the water toward the shore. This causes flood damage to areas along the coast. Surges can also happen on lakes.

Hurricanes can be tricky things. They can fool us into thinking that they have ended. The winds die down suddenly. We might think that the hurricane is over. But it's not! This is the "eye" of the storm. Here the winds are almost calm. It might even be sunny.

If you are in the eye of a hurricane, you are in the middle of it.
Watch out! The winds will start up again suddenly, and you want to make sure you're still in a safe place.

● This is what the eye of Hurricane Isabel looked like from space.

Chapter 6

Heat Waves

Summer doesn't only bring rain and thunderstorms. It also brings hot weather.

You may like hot, sunny days, but like many types of weather, too much of it can be a bad thing. Hot weather often brings heat waves, smog and **drought** [drowt].

People usually feel comfortable in a temperature that is around 22 degrees Celsius. But some summer days can get much hotter than that. A heat wave is when we have three days in a row that are hotter than 32 degrees Celsius. That can be very uncomfortable!

Why do we get heat waves? Hot days happen when cold air gets trapped north of us and can't move south to cool us off. If it gets stuck too long, then we get many days where it is very hot. The warm air just sits above us and doesn't move.

During a heat wave the air may be very humid. We use the word **humidity** to describe how much water there is in the air. When it's humid, our sweat can't evaporate and cool us down. That is why it feels hotter on a humid day.

When it gets too hot outside,
our bodies might overheat or we
may have problems breathing.

**How to stay safe and healthy
during a heat wave**

1. Drink lots of water.

2. Try to find shade or air conditioning.

3. Avoid too much exercise.

4. Always wear sunscreen and protective
clothing like a hat.

5. Rest after 30 minutes of outdoor play.

6. Don't let your parents leave any pets
in a car.

Many scientists believe that Earth
may be getting more heat waves
because of something called **global
warming.**

Our cars, trucks and power plants put chemicals into our air and this creates **pollution**. The pollution rises into the air and makes it hard for the Sun's heat to escape into space.

🔵 Can you see the difference? These are both pictures of Quebec City. One was taken on a clear day. The other was taken on a smoggy day.

The heat that is trapped causes Earth's temperature to rise. That is why it is called global warming.

Climate is the weather in an area over a long time. Many scientists believe that global warming is causing our climate to change faster than it should.

On hot days, you may have heard people talk about smog. Smog is actually two words made into one: smoke and fog.

Smog is pollution created by chemicals in our atmosphere. When the air is not moving, the pollution is trapped in one place. You might see a low, thin brown cloud. That is smog.

When an area doesn't get enough rain or snow for a long time we call this a **drought**.

Droughts can make heat waves even worse. Plants, animals and humans all need water to survive. But sometimes we don't get enough.

Droughts happen when water vapour doesn't get carried to the right areas at the right times. It may be because the weather is stuck in a certain pattern.

Droughts happen often on the Canadian Prairies. This is very hard on farmers who need to grow food.

In the 1930s the Prairies had many years of drought. The earth was very dry. Giant clouds of dust from the land blew across the Prairies.

The clouds would block out the Sun. People called these storms "black blizzards." It must have been pretty scary!

Recently we've had a lot of droughts. There were droughts in 2002 and 2003. In fact, the Prairies haven't been so dry in over 135 years!

The Dust Bowl Drought of the 1930s

Chapter 7

Wild Weather Facts

⚡ Lightning can travel at 140000 km per second. At that speed a rocket could go to the moon in three seconds!

⚡ In 1996 the amount of water that Quebec got in its flood in two days was the same as the amount of water that goes over Niagara Falls in four weeks!

Toronto's CN Tower gets hit by lightning about 75 times a year!

⚡ Canada's worst heat wave was in July 1936. The temperature in Toronto reached 41 degrees Celsius for three days in a row. It also got very hot in the Prairies. More than one thousand people across Ontario and the Prairies died.

⚡ If you want to know how far away a storm is, count the seconds between a lightning flash and thunder. For each second you count, the storm is 300 metres away. That is very close!
If they happen at the same time, the storm is right above you.

⚡ It's not true that lightning never hits the same place twice.

⚡ Fog is really just a low cloud. It is formed by tiny droplets of water that collect close to the ground.

⚡ A raindrop has about 15 million tiny droplets of water.

⚡ Tornadoes usually occur in the late afternoon or early evening.

⚡ The largest hailstone in Canada fell in Saskatchewan in 1973. It was as big as a softball!

⚡ The longest-lived hurricane in the Atlantic Ocean was Hurricane Ginger. It lasted 28 days!

⚡ In 1979 scientists started using male and female names to keep track of hurricanes. There are six lists of names, and a different list is used every year.

Canada's Most Deadly Tornadoes

◎ Regina, Saskatchewan — June 30, 1912

◎ Edmonton, Alberta — July 31, 1987

◎ Windsor, Ontario — June 17, 1946

◎ Pine Lake, Alberta — July 14, 2000

◎ Windsor, Ontario — April 3, 1974

◎ Barrie, Ontario — May 31, 1985

◎ Sudbury, Ontario — August 20, 1970

If a hurricane has caused a lot of damage, countries can ask to have a name removed. In 2004 Canada asked to have the name "Juan" taken off the list. It was the first time that Canada has ever done this.

Canadian Summer Weather Record Holders

Warmest place: Chilliwack, British Columbia

Driest city: Whitehorse, Yukon

Fewest sunny days: Prince Rupert, British Columbia

Hottest summer: Kamloops, British Columbia

Most thunderstorm days: Windsor, Ontario

Fewest thunderstorm days: Nanaimo, British Columbia

Sunniest city: Medicine Hat, Alberta

Glossary

Atmosphere: the mixture of gases that surrounds our planet

Climate: the weather in an area over a long period of time

Debris: the pieces of something that has been broken

Drought: a long period of time with no rain

Evaporation: when heat causes water to turn into a gas called water vapour

Global warming: the rise in Earth's air temperature caused by gases in the atmosphere; also called the "greenhouse effect"

Humidity: how much water vapour there is in the air around us

Meteorologist: a person who studies and predicts weather

Pollution: what happens when harmful chemicals are added to the land, water or air

Static electricity: a form of electricity that builds up in an object

Storm surge: a rise in water due to a storm

Tornado warning: a tornado has been seen; take shelter right away

Tornado watch: a tornado might happen in your area

Water vapour: a gas that is formed when water is heated; water vapour forms clouds